A LOOK AT U.S. HISTORY

THE TRAIL OF TEARS

BY BEATRICE HARRIS

Gareth Stevens PUBLISHING

CRASHCOURSE

Please visit our website, www.garethstevens.com. For a free color catalog of all our high-quality books, call toll free 1-800-542-2595 or fax 1-877-542-2596.

Library of Congress Cataloging-in-Publication Data

Names: Harris, Beatrice, author.
Title: The Trail of Tears / Beatrice Harris.
Description: New York : Gareth Stevens, [2022] | Series: A look at U.S. history | Includes bibliographical references and index. | Contents: Native Peoples on Native Lands -- The Indian Removal Act -- Choctaw, Creek, and Chickasaw Agreements -- The Seminole Fight Back -- Resisting Removal -- On the Trail -- The Trail of Tears -- A New Home -- After the Trail of Tears -- A Timeline of the Trail of Tears.
Identifiers: LCCN 2020014262 | ISBN 9781538266519 (library binding) | ISBN 9781538266496 (paperback) | ISBN 9781538266502 (set) | ISBN 9781538266526 (ebook)
Subjects: LCSH: Trail of Tears, 1838-1839--Juvenile literature. | Indians of North America--Southern States--Relocation--Juvenile literature. | Five Civilized Tribes--Relocation--Juvenile literature. | Cherokee Indians--History--Juvenile literature. | Cherokee Indians--Relocation--Juvenile literature.
Classification: LCC E99.C5 H26 2022 | DDC 975.004/97009034--dc23
LC record available at https://lccn.loc.gov/20200142

First Edition

Published in 2022 by
Gareth Stevens Publishing
111 East 14th Street, Suite 349
New York, NY 10003

Editor: Therese Shea

Photo credits: Series art Christophe BOISSON/Shutterstock.com; (feather quill) Galushko Sergey/Shutterstock.com; (parchment) mollicart-design/Shutterstock.com; cover, p. 1 courtesy of the Woolaroc Museum in Bartlesville, Oklahoma; p. 5 courtesy of the Smithsonian; pp. 7, 13 Interim Archives/Getty Images; p. 9 Michael Maslan/Corbis/VCG via Getty Images; p. 11 DEA PICTURE LIBRARY / De Agostini/Getty Images; pp. 13, 17 (seals) Morphart Creation/Shutterstock.com; p. 15 Turks /Shutterstock.com; p. 15 MPI/Getty Images; pp. 17, 19 courtesy of the Library of Congress; p. 21 (top) Denver Post via Getty Images; p. 21 (bottom) JNix/Shutterstock.com; p. 23 George Rose/Getty Images; p. 25 Nikater/Wikipedia.org; p. 27 © Historical Picture Archive/CORBIS/Corbis via Getty Images; p. 29 (sign) csfotoimages/iStock Editorial/Getty Images Plus; p. 29 Jacqueline Nix/iStock Editorial/Getty Images Plus.

Printed in the United States of America

CONTENTS

Words in the glossary appear in **bold** type the first time they are used in the text.

NATIVE PEOPLES ON NATIVE LANDS

At the start of the 1830s, at least 100,000 Native Americans lived in the southeast part of the United States. Their **ancestors** had lived on these lands for thousands of years. Yet, white settlers began claiming native lands for themselves.

MAKE THE GRADE

The southeast part of the United States includes the states of Georgia, Alabama, North Carolina, South Carolina, and Florida.

CHOCTAW PEOPLES PLAYING A BALL GAME

The native peoples who lived in the American Southeast were part of a larger group called Eastern Woodlands Indians. This group included the Cherokee, Creek, Chickasaw, Choctaw, and Seminole nations. At one point, British law had guarded these peoples' lands.

MAKE THE GRADE

In 1763, a British act stated settlers couldn't move onto Native American land west of the Appalachian Mountains. Many people **ignored** the act, however.

Native American land continued to be settled by non-natives. Many were looking for land to farm. Then gold was discovered in Georgia in 1829. More people rushed onto Cherokee land to try to find gold and get rich.

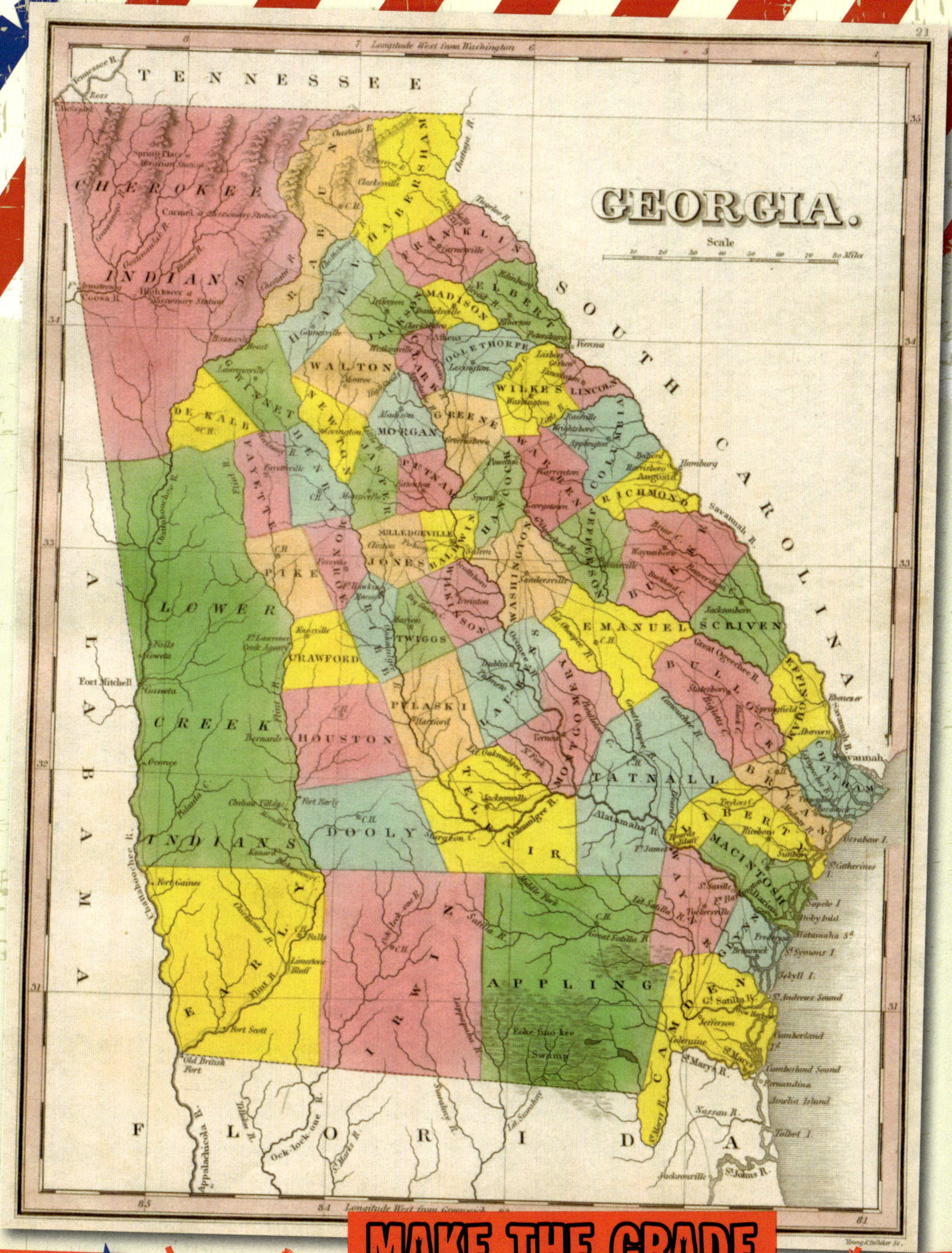

MAKE THE GRADE

Thousands traveled to Cherokee land in Georgia to find gold. Some called this the Great **Intrusion**.

THE INDIAN REMOVAL ACT

Many people in the United States wanted to take land from the Native Americans. President Andrew Jackson was in favor of this. In 1830, Congress passed the Indian Removal Act. It said Jackson could **negotiate** to move Native Americans to land west of the Mississippi.

MAKE THE GRADE

Andrew Jackson had been a U.S. army general before he was president. He fought against the Creek people of Georgia and Alabama and the Seminoles of Florida.

CHOCTAW, CREEK, AND CHICKASAW AGREEMENTS

The Choctaw and Creek signed agreements with the U.S. government. They were paid for their lands. The government helped them move west, but many died of illness, lack of food, and **exposure** on the way. The Chickasaw handled their own trip and had fewer problems.

CHOCTAW SEAL

CREEK SEAL

CHICKASAW SEAL

MAKE THE GRADE

"Creek" was the British name for the Muscogee people. Many Muscogee (or Mvskoke) still use both names.

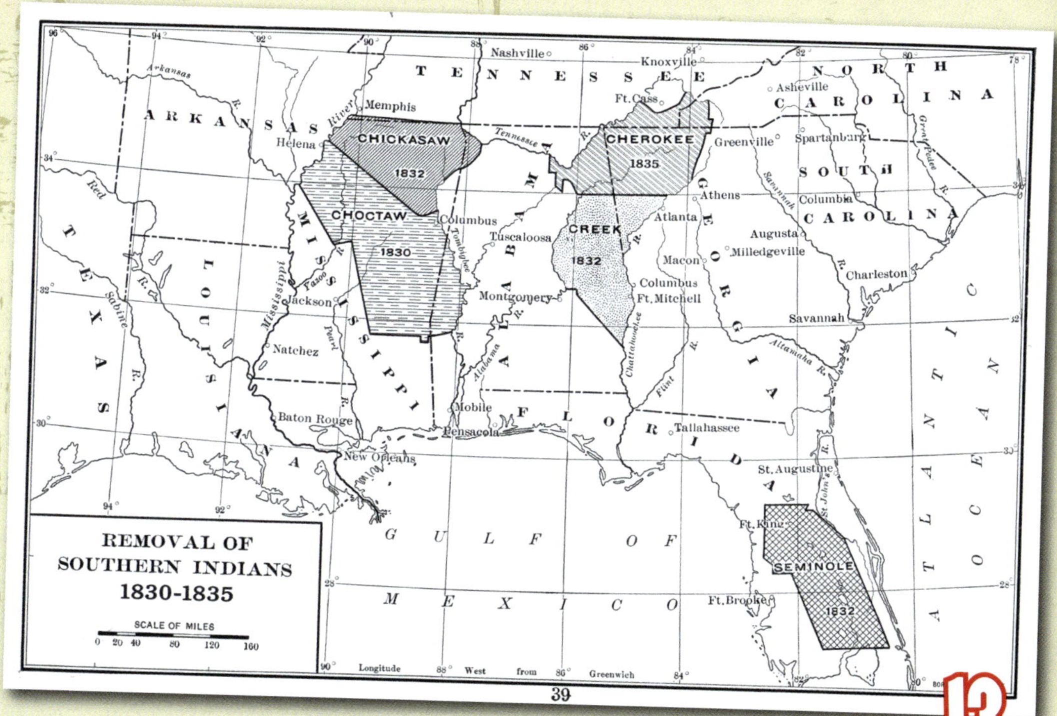

THE SEMINOLES FIGHT BACK

Some Seminoles made an agreement with the U.S. government to move west. However, other Seminoles said these people didn't **represent** them. The government tried to remove all Seminoles by force. This began the Second Seminole War, which lasted until 1842.

FLAG OF THE SEMINOLES OF FLORIDA

MAKE THE GRADE

Some Seminoles escaped the U.S. government. They remained in Florida while other Seminoles were forced to go west.

RESISTING REMOVAL

Some Cherokee agreed to move west. Others fought the Indian Removal Act with **lawsuits**. U.S. law saw the Cherokee as a nation, so many Cherokee expected their land rights to be respected. However, in 1838, the government began forcing them to move west.

CHEROKEE SEAL

MAKE THE GRADE

Cherokee chief John Ross (below) and 16,000 others said the agreement some Cherokee had signed with the government wasn't legal.

By 1838, Martin Van Buren was U.S. president. He sent about 7,000 soldiers led by General Winfield Scott to the Cherokee nation. The soldiers forced the Cherokee into camps, some for weeks. People stole from their homes. Then, the long journey west began.

MAKE THE GRADE

The land to which the Native Americans were taken was called Indian Territory. This map shows what the Indian Territory in today's Oklahoma looked like in 1887.

ON THE TRAIL

The journey from Cherokee land in Georgia to Indian Territory was about 1,200 miles (1,931 km). Many Cherokee were ill before their journey started. They didn't have the clothing or supplies they needed. Some took a water **route**. Others walked the whole way.

MAKE THE GRADE

Native Americans of the Northeast were also forced to move. They made up about one-third to one-half of all Native Americans who were moved from the East.

About 15,000 Cherokee were forced out of Georgia. Historians believe that at least 4,000 died on the way west. Illnesses killed many. Others died of **starvation**. The Cherokee people call the way "The Trail Where They Cried."

MAKE THE GRADE

About 1,000 Cherokee escaped before the move. Others walked back east. These Cherokee settled in North Carolina. Today they're called the Eastern Band of Cherokee Indians.

THE TRAIL OF TEARS

Today, the paths that the Native American nations of the Southeast took to the Indian Territory are called the Trail of Tears. Records suggest about 100,000 people were forced from their native lands and about 15,000 died on the journey west.

MAKE THE GRADE

Together, the paths of the Trail of Tears are more than 5,000 miles (8,047 km) long. They go through nine states: Alabama, Arkansas, Georgia, Illinois, Kentucky, Missouri, North Carolina, Oklahoma, and Tennessee.

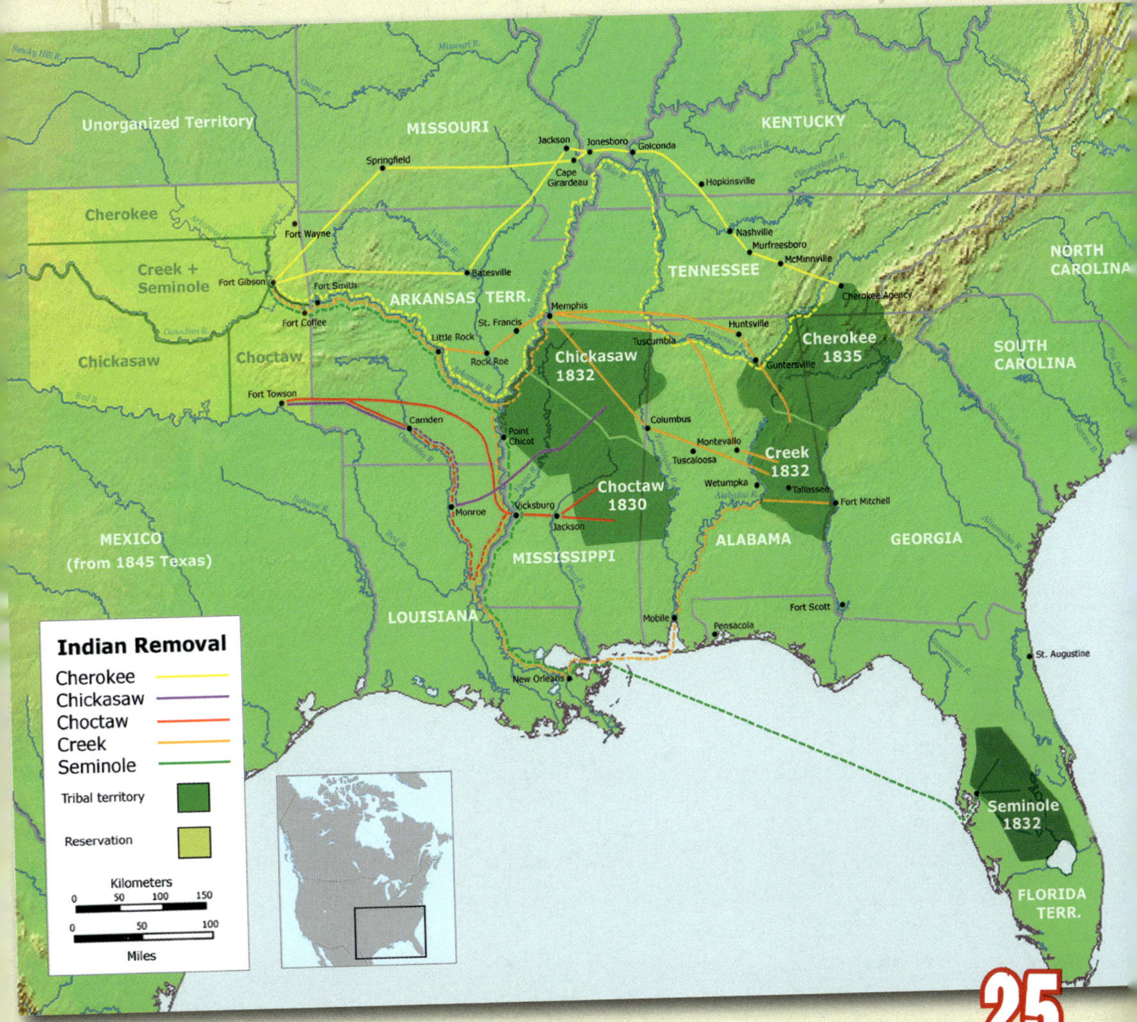

A NEW HOME

It wasn't easy for the eastern Native Americans to settle in Indian Territory. Many had been forced to leave their belongings behind, including farming tools. The U.S. government put them on lands that other Native Americans, such as the Plains Indians, called home.

MAKE THE GRADE

The Plains Indians weren't farmers. They were hunters and gatherers. At first, they **raided** what the U.S. government said were Chickasaw lands in Indian Territory.

AFTER THE TRAIL OF TEARS

The U.S. government promised Indian Territory would remain Native American land. However, the western half opened to settlers in 1866. In 1907, Indian Territory and Oklahoma Territory became the state of Oklahoma. However, the memory of the Trail of Tears lives on.

MAKE THE GRADE

In 1987, Congress made the Trail of Tears a National Historic Trail. People can follow it and remember what happened.

A TIMELINE OF THE TRAIL OF TEARS

1763
Great Britain passes a law to stop settlers from taking Native American land in the American Southeast.

1829
People find gold on Cherokee land in Georgia.

1830
The Indian Removal Act starts negotiations for removing Native Americans from the American Southeast.

1830
The Choctaw sign an agreement with the U.S. government.

1831
The lawsuit called *Cherokee Nation v. Georgia* is argued in the Supreme Court. The court rules against the Cherokee.

1832
The Chickasaw sign an agreement with the government.

1832
The Creek (Muscogee) sign an agreement with the government.

1832
Some Seminoles sign an agreement. Others disagree.

1835
The Second Seminole War begins.

1838
The Cherokee are forced from their homes on a deadly march to Indian Territory.

1839
The last group of Cherokee reaches Indian Territory. At least 4,000 Cherokee died on the way.

GLOSSARY

ancestor: a relative who lived long ago

exposure: the condition of being unprotected from bad weather

ignore: to take no notice of something on purpose

intrusion: the act of coming into a place where one isn't wanted or welcome

lawsuit: the way through which a court makes a legal decision to end a disagreement between people or groups

negotiate: to try to come to an agreement

raid: to suddenly attack

represent: to stand for or act for

route: a path that people travel

starvation: the act of suffering and dying because of a lack of food

FOR MORE INFORMATION

Books

Behnke, Alison. *A Timeline History of the Trail of Tears.* Minneapolis, MN: Lerner Publishing Group, 2016.

Schwartz, Heather E. *Forced Removal: Causes and Effects of the Trail of Tears.* North Mankato, MN: Capstone Press, 2015.

Websites

Trail of Tears
www.cherokeemuseum.org/archives/era/trail-of-tears
Find out more about the Trail of Tears and the Cherokee people on this website.

Trail of Tears
www.ducksters.com/history/native_americans/trail_of_tears.php
Read more about this terrible event in U.S. history.

Publisher's note to educators and parents: Our editors have carefully reviewed these websites to ensure that they are suitable for students. Many websites change frequently, however, and we cannot guarantee that a site's future contents will continue to meet our high standards of quality and educational value. Be advised that students should be closely supervised whenever they access the internet.

INDEX